Original title:
Tassels and Touch

Copyright © 2025 Creative Arts Management OÜ
All rights reserved.

Author: Penelope Hawthorne
ISBN HARDBACK: 978-1-80586-160-7
ISBN PAPERBACK: 978-1-80586-632-9

Emotions Entwined

In a world where socks have flair,
And mismatched shoes dance in air.
A cat with bows upon its head,
Turns the living room to a bed.

Bananas hanging from a tree,
Say hello to the little bee.
While funny hats roll down the street,
And every pet has tiny feet.

Shimmering Touchstones

A spoon that sings when in the pot,
And jellybeans that touch the hot.
Our laughter echoes, blocks on floors,
A battle fought with sharpened spoons.

Tickling toes and silly sings,
A dancing queen with colorful rings.
In every corner, joy anew,
As flashlights turn the night to blue.

Curled Edges of Memory

Old photos stuck to cheesy walls,
Dance about as laughter calls.
A sandwich that has grown a beard,
Brings giggles forth, especially weird.

The dog in socks, a sight to see,
Waltzes past with utmost glee.
Twirling cookies on the floor,
And gummy bears that roar for more.

Interwoven Paths

A park where trees wear fancy coats,
While ducks parade with little boats.
Each picnic squeaks with joyful bites,
As ants march on in silly fights.

Between the swings and laughter loud,
A kite flies high above the crowd.
With every joke and playful jest,
Our friendship ties, we are the best.

Whispers of Frayed Edges

In the corner, threads unwind,
Dancing quirks we daily find.
With every snag, a laugh erupts,
As chaos in fabric happily disrupts.

Socks mismatched, yet still a pair,
Stories woven, with room to spare.
Laughter hides in tangled threads,
Life's little mess, where humor spreads.

Threads of Connection

A string pulls tight, a bond so grand,
Like two left shoes that never planned.
In naps and snags, we find delight,
Two silly folks, in a tangled fight.

Bobbles puffing on knitted hats,
Silly puns from furball chats.
Weaving tales in clumsy style,
Life's a dance, let's laugh awhile!

Embracing the Adorned

Fringes flutter on a frock,
Ticklish charms that tick and knock.
In every fold, a giggle hides,
Revealing fun where fashion bides.

Catch the tassel, give it a twirl,
With every spin, we laugh and whirl.
Adorned in quirks, we stride with glee,
Life's a jest, come join the spree!

Caresses of Texture

Feathery fluff and scratchy wool,
A hug of fabrics, playful and full.
Each twist and turn, a giggling race,
In this cozy place, we find our space.

Bumpy, soft, like a cheeky grin,
Textures tease, let the games begin.
With every cuddly, goofy chat,
We embrace the fun with a tip of the hat.

Threads That Bind

In a world of knots and loops,
A cat plays with my favorite scoops.
Each thread a quirky little tale,
As I trip on my own shoelace trail.

Laughter echoes in every tug,
A grandma's sweater, a fashion shrug.
With every yank, my heart skips beats,
Life's a dance in messy feats.

Cascading Feelings

On a windy day, the scarf takes flight,
Swirling and twirling in sheer delight.
It wraps around me, then makes a run,
  I chase it down; oh, isn't this fun?

The neighbors chuckle from their lawns,
  As I prance like a bird in dawns.
  A belly laugh from the sun above,
Embracing chaos, that's what I love.

Fringed Whispers

Curtains flutter when secrets dance,
A playful breeze leads to romance.
Tipsy threads giggle in the breeze,
Winking at strangers, oh, such tease!

A yarn unravels, ties my shoe,
It sings a tune, "Have fun, it's true!"
Each fray a hint of joy and jest,
Life's a tapestry, we're truly blessed.

Delicate Threads

A sewing mishap turns quite bizarre,
Buttons flying like a shooting star.
With every stitch, I weave a tale,
Of silly moments to set the sail.

A ladybug lands on my knee,
As if to say, 'Hey, look at me!'
In every stitch, a giggle grows,
In tangled yarn, the laughter flows.

Swaying Silhouettes

In the breeze they dance and sway,
A funny jolt, a bright display.
With floppy hats and silly shoes,
They shuffle quick, they'll crack a ruse.

Laughter floats like feathers light,
Chasing shadows left and right.
In playful spins, they twist and bash,
A slapstick scene, oh what a clash!

Fringed Affection

They flutter 'round like tipsy friends,
In wobbly lines, the fun transcends.
With giggles shared and winks exchanged,
Such quirky charms, it's all arranged.

The world's a stage of silly plight,
Who tied these knots? What sheer delight!
With tangled ties, they'll make you grin,
A fringe of laughs that won't wear thin.

Tangled Sentiments

In playful knots, their paths entwine,
Dancing clumsily, oh so fine.
With every tug, they squeal and slide,
A comic twist; there's no more pride.

With whimsical spins and laughs galore,
They bounce along, asking for more.
A jolly mess of joy and cheer,
What a sight, they're always near!

Whispering Ribbons

They flutter soft like gentle chimes,
Humor wrapped in silly rhymes.
With every tease, they seem to shout,
These playful things, what's this about?

In a silly fight, they pull and tug,
Creating giggles, a raucous shrug.
They spin and swirl on steps so light,
A comic feast, pure delight!

Delicate Grasp

A tiny string, it slips and flies,
I catch it quick, yet something cries.
It dances round, oh what a show,
I try to hold it, but it won't slow.

With every tug, it gives a wink,
I laugh so hard, can barely think.
This little game, a hoot and holler,
It twirls away, I hear it swallow.

Intertwined Moments

In the tangled fun, we spin in glee,
You pull the left, I yank the free.
A jolly mess, a playful knot,
We laugh so loud, oh what a plot!

Around our fingers, chaos swirls,
It twists and turns with giggling twirls.
A comical chase, we run and dive,
In the flurry, we feel alive!

Elegance in the Tangle

Oh, this fine dance of loop and flair,
I twist my leg, you snatch my hair.
A waltz of whimsy, a charming fright,
We spin in circles, laugh with delight.

Each little tug, a clumsy grace,
A merry chase, we race and face.
So much comedy in every loop,
Together we form a silly troupe.

Frayed Memories

Once upon a time, we tried to weave,
It came apart, we couldn't believe.
With frayed ends flying, we had a ball,
The laughter echoed, we'd surely fall.

There's joy in chaos, a splendid sight,
We tease each other, oh what a night.
In memories fraying, we find our fun,
In tangled tales, we are never done.

The Touch of Fabric

Soft drapes dance with glee,
As they twist and twirl quite free.
A slip and slide, chaos reigns,
Snags on shoes lead to funny gains.

Fabrics whisper silly tales,
Of tangles and of messy trails.
Threads run wild, a knotty fight,
Who knew dressing could be so contrite?

A vest that sways from side to side,
Worn by a cat with so much pride.
Pants that squeak with every step,
Making everyone giggle and prep.

In the end, a fashion show,
Where fabrics act like they don't know.
Rolling laughter fills the air,
As outfits become a joyous affair.

Ethereal Textures

A scarf that floats on breezy whims,
Turns heads with a dance of spins.
Lacy layers, frilly and bold,
Taking clumsy turns like clocks of old.

Twirling socks in mismatched flair,
Socks that frolic without a care.
A shirt with sleeves that won't behave,
Hiding giggles, for it's quite a rave.

The fabric's quest to be the king,
Stuck in doors, learning to sing.
Elastic bands that snap and play,
Making everyone laugh all day.

In a world of undertones and hues,
Where threads create amusing views.
Texture games lead to hearty cheer,
With each faux pas, we find delight here!

Milestones in Fabric

Each hemline marks a blundered plot,
Where stitches flutter, perhaps forgot.
A cape that flies in a gusty breeze,
Strikes silly poses with utmost ease.

Button battles, oh what a scene,
As they pop off, it's quite a routine.
Lining lost with an awkward fold,
The dress, once fine, now turns bold and old.

Patchwork dreams patched with nonchalance,
Frayed edges take a comical stance.
As seams unravel, laughter breaks,
Creating tales, oh, what a mix-up makes!

Fashion faux pas become our flair,
Every stitch a giggle to share.
In the gallery of our fabric lore,
Milestones of humor, who could ask for more?

Tactile Dreams

Fuzzy hats on heads askew,
Tickling we see, oh how they grew.
A sweater that hugs too tight a frame,
A fight begins; it's all a fun game.

Fuzzy slippers on fancy feet,
Gliding, slipping, oh so sweet.
Like clouds on a runway's twisty lane,
Each step a giggle, fueled by the strain.

Fringes dance in a merry line,
Twisting and turning, oh how they shine!
Pants on the cat and socks on the dog,
The silliness grows, like mist in the fog.

In dreams of fabric, we laugh and play,
Each texture tells a tale, come what may.
For when the fabric flops and drapes,
We find the joy in these funny shapes!

Veils of Movement

In a dance of fluff and giggles,
Waving hands and sprightly wiggles,
Tripping over threads galore,
Laughter spills, we crave for more.

A playful tussle, who wears it best?
With flowy fabric, we're truly blessed,
But watch your step, oh what a fright,
Caught in a loop, we soar in flight.

Touching the Woven Dream

Fuzzy knits that tease the skin,
A tug of war, where do I begin?
Draped in colors that clash and blend,
I'll pull your thread, and we'll just pretend.

Threads that tickle and sometimes tease,
In our playful chaos, we find some ease,
Who knew a whim could twist so wild?
Each knot and loop, like a giggling child.

The Sway of Silken Décor

Swish and sway, a flouncy feat,
We trip and topple, oh, isn't it sweet?
A rope of dreams that dances about,
Pull it tight, it'll make you shout!

Cascading colors twirl in glee,
A fashion show for you and me,
Oh dear, why's your scarf in my hair?
Caught in the magic, a wild affair.

Fringes of Feelings

Fringe benefits of our playful spree,
I wear your laughter, you wear my knee,
A slapstick motion, what a surprise,
Who knew capes could cover our eyes?

A tangled mess, it's a charming sight,
We tumble and roll, oh, what a night!
With each little twirl, we sing and shout,
In a world of threads, joy's what it's about!

The Whisper of Fabric

In a shop where fabrics lie,
Bright patterns dance, oh my oh my!
Each roll a joke, with colors that tease,
A silk with a wink, that aims to please.

Linen giggles, wool plays shy,
Cotton's pranks make the mannequins cry.
A hushed confab of thread and seam,
It's a fabric world of whimsical dream.

Threads Unspoken

A snicker sews through seams unseen,
Where stitches plot in the in-between.
They pull and tug, a mischievous game,
Embroidered smiles, they have no shame.

The yarns unwound, they bend and sway,
Chatting softly about their day.
Knots of laughter in every fold,
Stitching in secrets, humorous gold.

Filigree of Feeling

A frilly hem knows all my quirks,
It sways and twirls, this dress it jerks.
Can you believe the tales it tells?
Of laughter stitched in rising swells?

Glittering threads weave joy and jest,
As fabric frolics, it knows no rest.
Each curl a chuckle, each line a grin,
A tapestry of giggles waiting to spin.

Fringes of the Heart

Fringes dangling, waving free,
In the breeze, they're wild with glee.
A dance of threads, a playful race,
A carnival on fabric's face.

With every wiggle, a joke unfolds,
Each sway a story, laughter it holds.
These tips and trails, with spirit imbued,
Bring frolicsome vibes to the mood's interlude.

Colors in Motion

Twirls of fabric dance and sway,
A rainbow flops on laundry day.
Tangles giggle in the breeze,
As socks play tag with utmost ease.

Ribbons wrestle in a heap,
Whisper secrets while I sleep.
Each shade jostles, makes a scene,
In a world of vibrant dreams.

Messy patterns run amok,
As buttons strut, a cocky flock.
A splash of hues in silly flight,
Turns mundane days to pure delight.

They swirl and spin, a silly spree,
Who knew shades could be so free?
With laughter stitched in every seam,
Life's a fabric, full of gleam.

The Warmth of Layers

I wear my clothes like a big hug,
Tangled fabric, a snuggly mug.
Every button tells a tale,
Of past adventures, wild and frail.

Layered chaos, just my style,
An outfit that can make you smile.
Socks that giggle, shirts that squeak,
Each one's charming, every week.

Bumping into friends, oh what fun,
My sleeves high-five, 'We've just begun!'
Scarves that dance and hats that cheer,
Together they conquer, year by year.

Fashion's a playground, wild and bright,
Each layer a buddy, dressed just right.
Jump into laughter, wrap it tight,
In this cozy mess, life feels so light.

Tactile Journeys

Fingers wander, exploring the scene,
Textures around me gleam and preen.
Cotton clouds and velvet dreams,
Each touch a giggle, bursting seams.

A silly poke, a gentle nudge,
Feathers tickle, won't budge.
Fuzzy socks and spongey shoes,
Giggles escape like the morning blues.

A fabric world where laughter reigns,
With every texture, joy sustains.
Yarns and threads weave tales quite grand,
A journey of senses, hand in hand.

Softness sparkling, bumping along,
With every texture, we hum a song.
Adventure awaits in feelings so bright,
In the world of stitches, we feel just right.

Embroidered Moments

Stitches laugh in a playful knot,
Every loop holds a little plot.
An embroidered tale, fun and bright,
Where threads play tag in the soft night.

Doodles of fabric crisscross apart,
A dance of colors, an artisan's heart.
Crafting giggles in creative ways,
Each little swirl a reason to praise.

Needles fondly weave the mirth,
Crafting patterns of joy and worth.
A patchwork of laughter, tales unfold,
In every design, adventures told.

Moments stitched with glee and care,
In the fabric of life, we find our flair.
So let's embrace this woven cheer,
Every embroidered memory, hold dear.

Woven in Gentle Light

In a café bright and warm,
A waitress spun with carefree charm.
Her apron danced with every move,
Like a boisterous star in a playful groove.

A customer spilled his drink with glee,
It splattered like a playful sea.
She laughed, wiped up with color and flair,
Creating a mosaic beyond compare.

In the corner, a painter watched the fun,
His brush strokes quick like a playful pun.
Each line a laugh, each hue a jest,
In this fabric of life, they both felt blessed.

So here we weave with giggles anew,
Life's little mishaps, a colorful view.
In gentle light, our hearts take flight,
With laughter woven, all feels right.

Edges of Affection

A kitten chased its fluffy tail,
While the dog just wagged, it seemed to hail.
On the sofa, hearts were knit,
In a patchwork of love, they'd freely sit.

A grandmother cackled at the sight,
As yarn rolled past in a gleeful flight.
With every knot, a chuckle arose,
In this home, warmth and laughter glows.

The fish bowl bubbles with silly cheer,
As the cat plans its sneaky career.
Paws tap and dance on the edge of fun,
In this colorful mess, we're never done.

Each stitch a giggle, each row a smile,
In the playful chaos, we stay awhile.
With edges frayed but hearts so bright,
Life's funny fabric, a pure delight.

Dancing Fibers

In the closet, garments pile high,
Jackets jive while scarves fly by.
A sock with stripes just took a leap,
While the hats all giggled, stirring from sleep.

In the living room, a rug takes the floor,
As shadows twist, with laughter to explore.
The couch whispers secrets, cushions in bliss,
The fibers all dance, not a moment to miss.

A mischievous foot pokes through the seam,
Creating a spectacle, like a funny dream.
With each little wobble, the fun escalates,
As the curtains wave back with cheeky traits.

So clothes hang loosely, unbothered by style,
In this joyful mess, we'll cherish a while.
They sway with the rhythm of life's crazy tune,
In fibers' embrace, we all swoon.

Soft Caresses of Color

A rainbow spilled through the window pane,
While brightly hued feathers danced in vain.
The chubby parrot squawked with delight,
At the artful display of colors in flight.

Crayons rolled under the giggling chairs,
As kids crafted rainbows without any cares.
With sticky fingers and paint-splattered feet,
Creative chaos made the day sweet.

A blender hummed with a fruity blend,
While kitchen towels played the perfect friend.
In pastel tones, they wiped away mess,
Adding laughter and color to the everyday stress.

So let's twirl through this dazzling hue,
With each soft caress, inspire something new.
Life's a canvas, and oh what a show,
In this playful patchwork, together we grow.

Fleeting Fingers

Fingers dancing in the air,
Like kites caught in a snare.
They wave and wiggle with glee,
Trying to grasp what's hard to see.

A pinch of fabric, a playful lift,
Creating chaos, a harmless rift.
Laughter blooms in every poke,
The art of jest, a gentleoke.

The joy of jesting, a wriggly show,
As fingers frolic and dance to and fro.
In silly antics, they often lose,
What came first? Who knows? Who'd choose?

So come catch the whimsy, join in the play,
Let those nimble digits sway.
We'll laugh till we practically fall,
In this game of jest, there's room for all.

Ribboned Emotions

Colors swirling, never quite still,
Like marshmallows tossed down a hill.
Each hue a giggle, each shade a shout,
Twisting and turning, there's joy all about.

With swirls and whirls, they bounce with glee,
Never forgetting how wild they can be.
A heartfelt tug or a cheerful sway,
These playful bands know how to play.

Oh, what a mess their vividness makes,
Like a cake with too many frosted flakes.
Yet amidst the laughter is friendship's thread,
Binding us gently, not leaving us dread.

So, let's twirl and spin with this bright delight,
Our emotions ribbed, taking flight!
With joy tangled up in every hue,
Together we'll make a colorful brew.

The Lure of Loose Ends

Those pesky threads just won't behave,
Twirling around like they want to rave.
A knot here, a tangle there,
It's a dance of fabric everywhere!

Hands reach out, trying to untwist,
Every knot leads to another twist.
They giggle and grin when fingers apply,
The test of patience; oh, how we sigh!

Each loose end has a quirky charm,
With a roll, a bounce—never a harm.
They wiggle and jiggle, full of flair,
Inviting chuckles while we declair.

In a world of knots, we seek the bright,
Finding laughter in each tangled sight.
So let's embrace this merry thread,
With laughter around, no need for dread.

Texture Beneath the Surface

Textures lurking, a playful tease,
Each crinkle and fold aims to please.
Like a handshake gone mad, it grabs at the air,
Unruly and wild, with nary a care.

Fingers searching for hidden delight,
While surfaces shimmer, ready to bite.
Each poke a giggle, each brush a jest,
In this fabric game, we feel so blessed.

Tickles and thrills as we explore,
Mysteries within that we long to adore.
A swipe here, a nibble there,
With everything swirling, there's joy to spare.

So let's dive deep into this cloth so grand,
Where textures await at every hand!
With laughter to guide us, let's wade through the fun,
In the fabric of life, we're never done!

The Untamed Weave

In a closet full of chaos, they dance,
Threaded limbs in a clumsy prance.
Ever tangled in the morning light,
A fashion show gone hilariously bright.

Hats askew and shoes misplaced,
The outfits all seem to be interlaced.
Legs are tied, and shirts once clean,
A runway brawl—the silliest scene.

Bobbing heads, with feathers on high,
A parrot lost in a sea of DIY.
With each yank and pull, giggles ensue,
Who knew clothing could cause such a zoo?

In a world where knots become style,
Laughter erupts; we walk the aisle.
The tangled tale of our wardrobe's game,
Is funny fashion without any shame.

Sensations in Bloom

Frills flutter like butterflies poised,
Each layer whispers secrets unvoiced.
Colorful chaos in a joyful spree,
The garden of fabric calls out to me.

Petals twirl and seams engage,
A blooming mess, a handmade stage.
With every stitch, we weave delight,
In the flower patch, oh what a sight!

Naps on tulips, drowsy bees hum,
Swatches smile while we're on the run.
The laughter of fabric, friends galore,
Springtime jesters, let's explore!

As daisies lace up in silly threads,
We prance around, tossing our heads.
A blooming quilt of laughter and cheer,
In this vibrant bower, we shed our fear.

The Poetry of Embellishment

Sequins shimmering like silly stars,
Dancing joyfully on glittering bars.
Patterns clash in outrageous delight,
A visual poem that sparks a light.

Glitter bombs burst with every move,
Rhymes of colors in a groovy groove.
Patches laugh and buttons sing,
In the tapestry where giggles cling.

Periwinkle hearts and orange moons,
Twisted tales that make us croon.
With every thread that pokes and jabs,
We craft our charm in silly drabs.

Embellished tales with a wink, a grin,
Foolish fabric, let the hijinks begin!
In this quirky verse, we find our glee,
The art of laughter, wild and free.

Velvet Whispers

Softly they sway, like secrets in night,
Velvet voices, oh, what a sight!
Each fold—a giggle, each twist—a grin,
Whispers of humor where silliness begins.

Crimson capes swirl as we chaotically flock,
Like ducks in attire that fails to unlock.
With every glide, the giggles arise,
A velvety ruckus beneath starry skies.

Cushiony shenanigans, pancake-shaped hats,
Wobbling around like befuddled cats.
The fabric flutters, and laughter takes flight,
In this frolicsome dance, all feels so right.

So let's twirl in comfort, fashion gone mad,
In a world of soft laughter, the best we've had.
With whispers of velvet, we weave our fate,
In hilarity's embrace, we celebrate!

The Elegance of Caress

In a dance of fluff and flair,
Sit, wiggle, giggle without a care.
Fringed laughter rises, bounces around,
Each playful flick makes hearts pound.

With playful loops and playful swings,
A ticklish breeze as mischief sings.
Oh, elegance found in silly grace,
Where every swish brings a smile to face.

So twirl your threads and let them sway,
Twisted jokes in a bright ballet.
The lightness rolls like summer rain,
In a world where whimsy reigns.

Forget the serious, bring on the jest,
In this fabric fun, we feel our best.
Laughter woven in every seam,
Caressing the soul, a joyous dream.

Hues of Connection

Colors clash in playful fight,
Mixing shades, oh what a sight!
Pink and blue, a wild affair,
Each hue laughs with light-hearted flair.

Spills of laughter in orange and green,
Every combination, a vibrant scene.
Brush strokes splash, giggles ignite,
Creating joy, painting pure delight.

Sketching memories with a wink,
This palette pulses, causing a sync.
Together we blend, find our way,
In a canvas of chuckles and bright array.

Every hue, a tale to tell,
In this jolly mix, we cast a spell.
Connection thrives with each playful stroke,
In shades of laughter, we gently choke.

Luminous Fringes

Glimmers dance on the edge tonight,
Swinging wildly, oh what a sight!
Fringes twirling with giddy delight,
In this glow, everything feels right.

Little flickers, a sparkly spree,
Radiating joy like a wild jubilee.
Every shimmer tells a funny tale,
Where light-hearted dreams set full sail.

With every wiggle, a twinkling shout,
These bright little strands leave us in doubt.
Do they dance, do they spin, need we know?
Their luminous frolics put on a show!

In the night's embrace, let's seize the chance,
Join the fringes in a happy dance.
Glowing together, oh what a mix,
In the fabric of laughter, let's find our fix.

Subtle Embrace

A gentle nudge, a smile so sly,
Whispers of fun that never die.
Hugs that wobble, like jelly on toast,
In this tender rumble, we love the most.

Come closer now for a friendly squeeze,
Wrapped in laughter, it's sure to please.
With every hug, a ticklish tease,
Moments like these, life's greatest keys.

Cozy chaos, where no one is shy,
Embraces fly like birds in the sky.
Each squeeze fuels joyous delight,
With every giggle, we soar to new heights.

So let's play together, in silly parade,
In this world of quirk, let's never fade.
In every embrace, joy finds its place,
Creating memories, woven with grace.

Unraveled Dreams

A wild yarn flew through the air,
Chasing cats without a care.
Puppies tangle in a heap,
While giggles rise, we barely sleep.

What a mess, a colorful sight,
Knots and loops, a crafty fright.
Grandma's knitting in a twist,
Her patterned chaos, we can't resist.

With every tug, a funny scene,
The laughter bursts, bright and keen.
A tale of threads gone quite awry,
As we weave mischief, oh my oh my!

Fuzzy threads that won't align,
A dance of dolls in strings divine.
We play like fools with every flare,
In our jumbled world, we do declare!

Veils of Sensation

A curtain sways, a soft embrace,
Ticklish fingers, a wild race.
Draped in colors, bold and bright,
We twirl around, what a delight!

A windy day, a fluttering kiss,
Whirling skirts, can't help but miss.
We dip and dive in laughter's wave,
As fabric flies, oh how we rave!

Jokes unfold like ribbons tossed,
In this frolic, no one's lost.
With every flounce, a silly dance,
Revealing giggles, give it a chance!

The world's a game, in fabric spun,
Where fancies loom and joy's begun.
As veils unfold, we can't resist,
This playful dance, our secret tryst!

Threads of Memory

Each memory's a colorful thread,
Woven tales from days long fled.
A laugh caught in a half-spun race,
As we trace back, our silly face.

Cartwheels and mishaps fill the loom,
A tug of joy in every room.
From yarn of childhood tangled tight,
We weave our stories, pure delight.

Old friends laughing, hands entwined,
Each twist and turn, fate aligned.
With every knot, a tale to share,
In threads of gold, we breathe the air.

So grab the spool, let laughter flow,
In every mishap, joy will grow.
Together we stitch a life so bold,
With threads of memory, laughter unfolds!

Textures of the Heart

A patchwork quilt of laughter bright,
Woven with quirks and pure delight.
Each square tells tales, a story spun,
In silly moments, we find our fun.

Furry cushions and straws aflight,
A toddler's giggle in morning light.
Tickles and jests, oh what a blend,
In textures soft, our joys transcend.

Confetti jokes, a playful tease,
Mixing colors like a breeze.
The fabric of life—so wild, so free,
With textures warm, our hearts agree.

In every fold, a happy jest,
Life's a party, we're truly blessed.
So share a grin, let laughter chart,
These funny shapes, the textures of the heart!

The Dance of Edges

Threads are twirling in a swirl,
Edges flapping, a merry whirl.
Buttons bouncing, quite a show,
Fabric giggles, oh what a glow!

A hem that trips on a shoe so bright,
In this dance, we lean, take flight.
A seam that's loose, just say it's wild,
In the chaos, we're just each other's child.

Laces twisting, all askew,
Ribbons racing, who knew?
A stitch mislaid, a funny plight,
Laughter echoes, what a sight!

Come sway with me, we'll twine and twirl,
With every spin, our worries unfurl.
In this laughter, we freely roam,
In every edge, we find a home!

Softness in Between

A blanket folded, oh so plush,
Cushions bouncing in a rush.
Pillows puffing in delight,
Whispers soft as clouds take flight.

Underneath the quilt, a secret lies,
Where laughter hides and joy can rise.
Every fold hides a playful grin,
In this warmth, the fun begins!

Buttons pop with a funny sound,
In this soft, snug world, life's unbound.
Tickling toes beneath the sheets,
With every wiggle, joy repeats!

Embrace the fluff and squishy cheer,
Where fabric hugs, and there's no fear.
In the cozy night, we will scheme,
For fun and laughter are the dream!

Echoes of Fabric

Whispers of cloth in merry tones,
Ripples rustling like playful cones.
Scarves that swoosh, a lively fuss,
Echoes bouncing, just for us!

A tapestry of jokes in threads,
We weave laughter as the day spreads.
Every fringe tells a tale so bright,
Stitching giggles in the fading light.

Fabrics clapping with every cheer,
They shake and shimmy, so sincere.
A hem that dances, curly and spry,
With every movement, we can't say why!

After the play, with smiles wide,
Each fabric holding our fun inside.
So let them echo as we go,
In every fold, our laughter will grow!

Gentle Cascades

Ripples flowing down the seam,
Like water gliding in a dream.
Curtains flutter, a playful wave,
Cascading joy, we willingly crave.

A scarf that flops, quite the sight,
With every movement, pure delight.
Fringes drip with playful grace,
In this dance, we find our place.

Ruffles tumble, a fluffy dive,
Each layer adds to the jive.
Softly crashing, giggles blend,
Where playful waves never end!

So come and frolic, sway this way,
In cascades of joy, we'll play.
With gentle rolls of fabric fun,
We'll laugh together, one by one!

The Dance of Fiber

In a world of fluffy threads,
They wiggle and squirm, like little dreads.
Each twist and twirl, a clumsy spree,
A yarn ballet, just wait and see!

With colors bright, they jive and roll,
Deadpan faces, but that's the goal.
A stitch in time, a sock gone wild,
Oh, look! It's dancing, just like a child!

Pompoms bounce, they leap and shout,
Arguing who can fall about.
Tangled up in playful glee,
Who knew string could be so free?

A ball of fluff takes center stage,
Winks at the crowd, a mouth agape.
Each snip and clip, a fresh routine,
Who knew fibers could be so keen?

Echoes in the Fabric

In the closet, whispers spread,
Fabrics gossip, now that's not dead.
Silk prattles with denim's snark,
While cotton's laughing in the dark.

Ribbons shimmy down the seam,
Raucous laughter, a wild dream.
Polka dot silk dares to compete,
With stripes who think they're pretty neat.

Fuzzy socks declare a war,
On smooth threads that seek to score.
'You're too soft!' one fabric sings,
'And all your charm is merely flings!'

But in this playful, woven world,
Every hue and thread is swirled.
Echoes bounce from shelf to shelf,
A fabric riot, laugh for self!

Caresses at the Edge

Furry fingers tease the seams,
Tickling edges, oh what dreams!
A quilt giggles with every fold,
Gladly sharing secrets untold.

Velvet whispers, catching eyes,
While burlap rolls with hearty sighs.
Oh, the ruckus just won't quit,
When fibers meet, they laugh and flit.

A sudden fray, a playful scrape,
"Don't pull! This isn't tape!"
The edges wriggle, trying to stand,
In this party, it's quite unplanned.

With crafty snips and frayed delight,
They spin and twirl, all through the night.
Sewing chaos, which one to choose?
Caresses here will amuse, amuse!

Textured Embrace

A fluffy hug, a knitted twist,
Textures mingle, can't resist.
Corduroy in a goofy dance,
And fuzzy fleece just loves the chance.

A quilted heart, with pompoms bright,
Thickness tickles, oh what a sight!
Velcro's snicker, "I'm well adhered,"
While lace rolls eyes, "You're far too weird!"

The playful clash of textures bold,
Bringing warmth when nights turn cold.
Each fiber prances with a grin,
In a comical tactile din.

Embracing quirks, they laugh and tease,
In delightful chaos, they aim to please.
A tapestry of joy, we see,
In a world of fibers, wild and free!

Frayed and Focused

The sweater shrank, it fits the cat,
A quirky style, just look at that!
With sleeves so short, they barely exist,
Our fashion sense has gone amiss.

We twirl and shimmy, give it a shake,
A dance-off challenge, make no mistake!
In mismatched socks, we strut with glee,
Laughing at how wild we can be.

Stitching thoughts with bits of flair,
A tangled mess, but do we care?
With each odd knot, we create a scene,
Wearing our laughter like a queen.

So here we are, a silly crew,
With fabric thoughts and visions askew.
Unraveled dreams, we wear with pride,
In this odd world, we'll take a stride.

Textures of Togetherness

In the cupboard lies our finest thread,
A jumbled heap, it fills with dread.
Yet through the chaos, friends do cheer,
Creating wonders that bring us near.

With every tug and every pull,
Our secret formula feels so full.
Like sticky tape or mismatched pairs,
We make it work, despite our flares.

A funky quilt, all patched and bright,
Colors colliding, an odd delight.
We laugh at blobs, we giggle too,
Together, there's nothing we can't do.

In this wild mess, we've found a rhyme,
Each little quirk, we call it prime.
In joyful knots, we weave our song,
Finding the humor where we belong.

Threads of Intimacy

Two socks ambush a playful foot,
In this dance, we take a hoot.
A tangled love, quite out of place,
Yet in each twist, we find our grace.

With stringy tales we spin anew,
Silly whispers, just us two.
In our cozy den of yarns and dreams,
We tickle hearts with wild schemes.

Each loop we form, it brings us close,
In our woven world, we proudly boast.
We snicker as we trip and trip,
But hand in hand, we've got this grip.

Through frayed edges and silly glares,
We paint our moments, love declares.
In chaos bright, our bond will shine,
With every knot, your hand in mine.

Weaving Emotions

A fabric riot, wild and free,
Colors clash, oh can't you see?
Each strand we pull, a giggle here,
Creating memories, oh so dear.

With braided laughter and silly ties,
We forge connections, no surprise.
Through snags and tangles, we'll unwind,
A playful dance of heart and mind.

Let's throw in sparkles, and maybe a clown,
Twist those fibers and spin around!
In this mad art, we find our cheer,
With each odd pattern, you are near.

So wrap me up in your funny folds,
Together we'll weave our stories bold.
In every stitch, a smile we'll share,
In this patchwork life, we care.

Caressing Colors

In a world where hues collide,
Dancing shades take us for a ride.
A pink that tickles, a green that laughs,
The canvas giggles, crafting gaffes.

A purple wink, a yellow grin,
Colors that play, they turn us thin.
With every stroke, a chuckle erupts,
As rainbow jokes break from our cups.

Patterns prance on fabric's plane,
Swirling, twirling like crazy trains.
Each splash of fun, a playful tease,
Who knew colors had such expertise?

So grab your brush, come paint your mood,
Add a sprinkle of joy, a splash of food.
In this quirky world where laughter's bold,
Colors frolic as stories unfold.

Woven Whimsy

In the loom of life, threads entwine,
A tapestry of jokes, oh so fine.
Each yarn a giggle, tightly spun,
Binding together our funny run.

A stitch of laughter, a knot of cheer,
Weaving our stories, oh so dear.
With every pull, a twist of fate,
Creating smiles, it's never too late.

The fabric sighs, it's full of jokes,
A patchwork of wisdom from a bunch of folks.
With patterns that wiggle, and seams that play,
Our hearts are stitched in a quirky way.

So let your colors collide and bloom,
In this whimsical quilt, we find our room.
Laughter's the needle that threads us tight,
In this woven whimsy, we find delight.

Talismans of Emotion

In pockets deep, we carry charms,
Each little trinket brings us warm.
A bobble here, a jingle there,
Magic's in giggles, floating in air.

The baubles wink, they play their part,
Each token, a key to the heart.
From shiny stones to toys that squeak,
Their silly antics are what we seek.

When life gets dull and colors fade,
These precious gems throw a parade.
They twirl and twist, they bounce around,
In our laughter, their joy is found.

So keep your trophies of laughter near,
These talismans wise will draw us near.
With a pinch of fun and a dash of grace,
Our hearts will dance, and we'll find our place.

Threads of Light

In the fabric of dreams, we find our way,
Threads of bright laughter lead the play.
Each glimmering strand, a story unfolds,
As we stitch our mischief, in patterns bold.

A golden thread brings a wink of fate,
While silver lines encourage a mate.
Colors weave tales, sweet and spry,
As giggles float softly, oh my, oh my!

With every flicker of joyful lights,
We spin our yarns on whimsical nights.
Stitches of fun and frolics galore,
Turn ordinary moments to legendary lore.

So gather your threads, let's make a delight,
In this tapestry woven with beams so bright.
For in the fabric, with laughter in sight,
Together we shine, like stars in the night.

The Art of Hanging Threads

Upon my curtain rod they sway,
Fringed and playful in their play.
One's too high, one's too low,
A wobbly dance, oh what a show!

They twirl and twist without a care,
Each knot a giggle in the air.
Mom says, 'Hang them straight and neat!'
But who can stop this thread's retreat?

Some dangle low, some curl up high,
Like acrobats in a lazy sky.
A jolly mess, a vibrant sight,
These threads of joy, oh what delight!

Be it a leap or a little spin,
My playful strings pull me in.
With every swing, I laugh and shrug,
Who knew decor could give a hug?

Adrift in Softness

Fluffy clouds and cozy fluff,
Wrapped in warmth, oh that's enough!
I plunge my hands in sheer delight,
Like a kid on a snowy night!

Pool noodles and pillows collide,
Softness takes me for a ride.
I bounce upon this bouncy space,
Endless giggles in this place.

Lopsided cushions start to cheer,
'Come join us, dear, have no fear!'
I tumble in and wiggle free,
A hilarious hide-and-seek jubilee!

Every poke, tickle and tease,
Leaves me giggling, oh what a breeze!
In this realm of fluffy glee,
I find my joy, come play with me!

A Tangle of Sensations

Bouncing threads in a playful twist,
One's around my foot, oh how it kissed!
I step and trip on floppy scraps,
A circus act with all the laughs!

Whirs and whirls without a thought,
Jumbled feelings that I've caught.
Each loop and swirl makes me grin,
In this jumbled mess, let's begin!

My friends join in, oh what a scene,
Laughter shared, a silly routine.
We tangle up and make a pile,
With every twist, there's a new style!

In this patchwork of pure fun,
I'll wear my chaos like the sun.
Unraveled joy, come take a peek,
Join the adventure, it's quite the freak!

The Balance of Decoration

A swing and sway from side to side,
Like a dance party, full of pride!
My decor's in a vibrant spin,
Chandeliers grinning, let's begin!

One bobbles left, the other right,
A hanging jig that feels just right.
I try to balance, hold my breath,
But laughter's what I love the best!

Pompoms giggle and so do I,
Trying to keep the rhythm high.
Caught in a whirlwind, what a sight,
This goofy show of pure delight!

As colors clash and bulge of flair,
I find my joy, just floating there.
In this quirky dance of fate,
The balance tips – oh isn't it great?

Chords of Tenderness

In a world of knots and strings,
A tickle here, a giggle rings.
With every pull and playful tug,
We dance around, all snug as a bug.

Laces flying, a feathery chase,
Mittens mischief, what a race!
Giggles echo in each silly bind,
Crafting memories, wonderfully unrefined.

Bows untied, a comical spree,
Who knew threads could set us free?
With every stitch, a twist of fate,
A fabric friendship that feels first-rate.

So let's wrap up in this soft delight,
And laugh until we hug too tight.
In a tapestry of fun we find,
The whirly threads that intertwine.

Vibrant Connections

A burst of colors, a sprightly scene,
Each swirl and twirl is fresh and keen.
Dancing fibers, a playful spree,
Winking at you, and winking at me.

The wild yarns, with tales to tell,
Jokes embedded, they weave so well.
Threads of laughter, oh what a show,
Bright threads bound to make us glow.

In quirky knots, hilarity brews,
These playful ties are simply ruse!
Pull one end, and out pops a grin,
Who knew a tie could make us spin?

So here's to colors and frolics galore,
With vibrant threads that we adore.
Let's link our hearts in this silly blend,
For every twist, is a giggling friend.

Sensations in Texture

Scratchy, smooth, a fuzzy mishap,
Each gripping feel is a joyful clap.
Twirls of velvet, bumps that tease,
Textures that giggle, a playful breeze.

A tickle here, a scratchy woof,
Fuzzy slippers goofing in their goof.
Grab a corner, let's tickle the air,
Who knew feeling could be so rare?

Slippery silk in a tangled mess,
A delightful touch, oh what a stress!
We swaddle ourselves in absurd delight,
Every square inch turning bright.

With every texture, a spark of fun,
Each little touch becomes a pun.
So let's roam wild in this playful blend,
And cherish each feel from start to end.

Weaving Bonds

Threads interlace, a comical band,
Linking together, hand in hand.
With every twist, a laugh aligns,
Creating moments that brightly shine.

A goofy knot, a messy affair,
Tangles of laughter linger in the air.
With every loop, a fond embrace,
Binding us in this silly space.

Frayed edges and patterns that tickle,
Every pull brings a chuckle and giggle.
Together we weave, in mismatched glee,
Crafting connections as wild as can be.

So let's merge our threads like never before,
In this weaving of love and so much more.
A tapestry of joy, where fingers engage,
Laughing together, we set the stage.

Patterns of Silence

In rooms where whispers tread so light,
A sock caught whispers, oh what a sight!
Laughter between chairs begins to creep,
  As giggles settle in, we choose to leap.

The cat in the corner gives a sly grin,
Chasing the echoes, where do we begin?
A pie on the table seems to wail,
  Scraps of laughter follow like a tail.

In the crazy mess, thoughts rise and dip,
Like noodles on forks in a glorious trip.
What's said in silence? Questions abound,
  In this quiet circus, where joy is found.

So here we dance, in the hush of the night,
With socks as our partners, oh what a plight!
The patterns we weave in a fabric of fun,
Are the secrets we share when the day is done.

Hues of Love

In pots of paint, a story unfolds,
A brush strokes laughter in vibrant folds.
Dancing with colors, what a delight,
Each hue a chuckle, glowing so bright.

With splashes of red and some lime green,
We giggle and swirl, what a silly scene!
A rainbow of smiles, we splash all around,
In this palette of joy, our hearts are unbound.

What if blue tried to flirt with the pink?
Could yellow jump in and steal the blink?
Each canvas a canvas of stories untold,
In this colorful mess, we watch love unfold.

So paint your hearts, let the laughter arise,
In hues of delight that light up the skies.
With every brushstroke, we add to our cheer,
In this wacky gallery, love's always near.

The Dance of the Fringe

In the corner of rooms, fringes do sway,
With a jiggle and laugh, they brighten the day.
Curtains like party hats jump to attention,
Every sway is a giggle, pure joy's invention.

A rug with regrets tries to slip on by,
With a dance of disaster, it gives a shy cry.
What if the lampshade joins in the fun?
A waltz with a shadow beneath the sun!

The brooms in the closet start to complain,
As we dance with the mop, go against the grain.
With laughter and twirls, the fringe takes a stand,
In a whimsical show, we all lend a hand.

So let us twirl with fringes and more,
In this merry ballet, that we all adore.
With each playful sway, we echo a song,
In this funny dance, we all belong.

Delicate Jingles

Tiny bells chime as we quietly creep,
Through rooms filled with chuckles, a secret we keep.
Each jingle a whisper, oh what a thrill,
A symphony of giggles that time cannot kill.

Our shoes tap lightly on the floor's soft beat,
Dancing in silence, a playful retreat.
With jingles and giggles, we make quite a show,
As the cat joins in, with a bounce and a flow.

In the middle of jokes that tickle and tease,
The jingles ring out, with the greatest of ease.
A chorus of laughter, a magical spell,
In this orchestra of fun, we all can't help but dwell.

So gather around, let the merriment lift,
In this dainty ensemble, laughter's the gift.
With delicate chimes and joyous cheer rendered,
In this hilarious concert, our hearts are engendered.

Patterns of Affection

In a room full of strings, I trip and I fall,
My balance is shaky, I'm laughing through all.
With a swirl of bright colors, the yarn starts to play,
I'm tangled in friendship, hip-hip-hooray!

A cat on my lap, just plotting my fate,
She pounces on fabric with glee at such rate.
As I weave through the chaos, a thought crossed my mind,

In this dance of the silly, true joy I will find.

Each knot is a giggle, each loop a delight,
Woven moments of laughter, oh what a sight!
I might get all knotted, but hey, that's okay,
Life's a riotous game, my dear friend, let's play!

So here's to the patterns, we love and adore,
With threads of our stories, there's always much more.
Let's spin a great yarn, together we scheme,
In this fabric of antics, we'll live out our dream!

Soft Threads of Time

With cushions of comfort, we bounce on the floor,
Silly adventures, who could ask for more?
Stitching our moments with laughter and cheer,
In this quilt of existence, no worries appear.

The clock ticks in rhythm, a dance out of tune,
I wore mismatched socks and sang to the moon.
But time is a fabric, unspooling in fun,
Each second a thread, weaving joy on the run.

With patterns so bright, like polka dot skies,
We tangle our stories, oh how time flies!
The fluff and the giggles, they bubble and bloom,
In each soft embrace, we banish the gloom.

So let's roll in the fibers, of mirth and of glee,
For life's woven memories are shared you and me.
Every twist has a tale, every thread has a rhyme,
In this hodgepodge of fun, we'll dance through all time!

Subtle Echoes

Whispers of laughter, they ripple like streams,
In a quilt of odd sounds, a chorus of dreams.
I snort while I giggle, it's quite a delight,
These echoes of joy make the world feel so bright.

With every small blunder that brings laughter near,
The soft clink of spoons makes the atmosphere clear.
We fumble through dinner, with sauce on our face,
In this playful mishap, we find our own grace.

A nudge and a wink, oh how we collide,
Each chuckle a thread in the fabric of pride.
These echoes of fun float around like a breeze,
In the symphony of smiles, let's dance with such ease.

We sewed our tomorrows with stitches of cheer,
Each hint of a giggle, a sound that we hear.
Subtle yet loud, in the best of our days,
The echoes of laughter will guide us always!

Texture of Love

Oh, the fuzzy reminders of hearts intertwined,
A patchwork of moments, divinely designed.
We toss silly quips like confetti in air,
Each gesture a hug, we joyously share.

With mischief and fun, we fold and unfold,
Our bond is a fabric, a story well told.
The texture of laughter, the pattern of grace,
In this game of charades, we find our own space.

A playful embrace, a tickle, a tease,
Every thread that we weave is a spark of sweet ease.
From socks of the brightest to hats that don't fit,
We dance in this rhythm, oh isn't life lit?

So here's to the fibers that color our days,
In the joyous expressions, our hearts will amaze.
With patterns that shimmer and textures that sing,
In the tapestry of love, we've got everything!

Vibrant Strands

In the closet, a riot does bloom,
Stripes and polka dots chase away gloom.
A sock on the floor, a hat on a chair,
It's a fashion parade; you'd laugh at the flair.

Fringes dangling like jolly old friends,
Their wild antics could drive one to bends.
A sneeze and a tangle, oh what a sight,
This wardrobe's a party, oh what pure delight!

Sashes that wiggle, oh what do they know?
They ripple and laugh with a glamorous show.
Who knew a belt could be such a clown?
It twirls and it flips, never wears a frown!

With a flick and a swirl, each layer is free,
A ruckus of colors, just like a bee.
So let's dance with the hues all around,
In this silly closet, fun knows no bound!

Embracing Colors

A pink polka dot scarf screams with glee,
It wraps round my neck, as proud as can be.
Neon and pastel, a marvelous mix,
They tease and they play, they're quite the fix!

The layers will hug me like a warm pie,
Bouncing around like they're ready to fly.
When I trip on my shoe, they giggle a lot,
A comedy show? Why yes, quite the plot!

With every new layer, a new laugh appears,
The fabric is snickering, tickling ears.
A bangle will jingle, a pom-pom will cheer,
They dance on my toes, full of silly good cheer!

Oh, how they shimmer, they sparkle with fun,
In this playful race, we all become one.
Colors embracing, a carnival day,
In stitches and giggles, we frolic and play!

Filaments of Heart

A thread pulled tight, it tickles my soul,
Each strand whispers secrets, as I lose control.
Woven together in a laughable heap,
A playful ensemble, where joy's never cheap.

Buttons that bounce, with personalities bright,
They dance on my shirt, oh what a delight!
A mishap or two, they're not shy, you see,
When I try to button, they burst out in glee!

With fibers that shimmy, they laugh and they sway,
Every little fray tells stories at play.
Who knew that my outfit could be so absurd?
In the land of the silly, strange things go unheard!

With feathers and fluff, my ensemble's alive,
A party of textures, oh how they thrive!
This whimsical wardrobe makes everyday spark,
In filaments of laughter, I leave my mark!

The Art of Fringes

Fringes that wiggle, oh what a delight,
They sway like party guests, ready to bite!
A dance on my shoulder, a jig in the air,
Each flick of the fabric is filled with fair flair.

When a breeze takes a chance and gives them a toss,
They twirl and they swirl like the boss of the gloss.
Adding to my outfit, a raucous parade,
In my wardrobe of wonders, mischief is made!

Tassel-y creatures, they tease and they play,
With colors that pop in the cheeriest way.
Ribbons that ripple like laughter untold,
They take me on adventures, both silly and bold.

A bow here, a thread there, everybody frays,
When we dress up in joy, every inch of us sways.
In the art of the fringe, we find endless fun,
With laughter and play, the day's just begun!

Gentle Gestures

In the land of fluffs and frills,
A playful tug brings out some thrills.
Socks are dancing, look at them sway,
As the cat joins in, in a fluffy ballet.

Twisting and twirling, a wild parade,
Banana peels fly as laughter cascades.
Up on the shelf, a rogue mitten slips,
And falls on the floor with some dramatic flips.

Cousins reunited, knitting on keys,
Each instrument strums like a tickled breeze.
As yarns entangle in silly embrace,
Their giggles echo in this happy space.

Colors of Connection

A rainbow of ribbons, the twirls and the knots,
They giggle and bounce like dancing robots.
With every pull, a new shade appears,
And the pompoms shake off their yarny fears.

A bright purple string takes the lead,
While the green one whispers, "Oh, indeed!"
Together they prance, doing the conga,
While blue digs out snacks from a plushy longa.

Pineapple hats bobbing on heads,
As kaleidoscope chaos spreads on the threads.
In this merry mess, connections ignite,
With every embrace, pure delight takes flight.

The Dance of Threads

Strings entwined in a wobbly row,
They shimmy with laughter, don't you know?
With pom-poms leading, they all take their turn,
In a whirl of colors, their edges do churn.

A tug at the end, oh! What a sight,
A yarn ball rolls wrong, takes off with fright.
One prickly needle shivers with glee,
As the dance floor is set for a wild jubilee.

Fluffy pals twirl under disco lights,
In a swirl of fabric, oh what delights!
They leap and they spin, as fibers unwind,
In the house of hilarity, joy's intertwined.

Embraces of Yarn

A hug that is fuzzy, a squeeze full of zest,
In a world of fluffballs, you get the best!
Flannel is giggling, in the corner it prances,
While a squeaky toy joins in for the dances.

Under the table, the kitten does lurch,
Cuddling the cushions in an affectionate search.
Each twist and each turn, is a moment to save,
In the comedy of weaving, we all misbehave.

A yarn knot gets tangled, what a sight to see,
Everyone's roaring, it's pure jubilee!
With each goofy grin, connections grow wide,
In this playful embrace, all chaos is tied.

www.ingramcontent.com/pod-product-compliance
Lightning Source LLC
Chambersburg PA
CBHW070304120526
44590CB00017B/2558